CONTRIBUTORS

John E. Allen

Neil Ardley

Sue Becklake

Robert Burton

Barry Cox

Jacqueline Dineen

Plantagenet Somerset Fry

Bill Gunston

Kaye Orten

Tom Williamson

Tom Wright

ARTISTS

Jim Bamber

Dick Eastland

Claire Eastman

Phillip Emms

Dan Escott

Elizabeth Graham-Yool

Colin Hawkins

Eric Jewell

Barry Salter

John Sibbick

Raymond Turvey

Photo Credits:
I.M. Ball; Biofotos;
California Institute of Technology;
Douglas Dickins; Michael Holford;
Matt Irvine; NASA; Novosti Press Agency;
Photri; Space Frontiers;
U.S. Naval Observatory; Zefa.
Front Cover; Space Frontiers

CHIEF EDUCATIONAL ADVISER

Lynda Snowdon
Infant School Headteacher

TEACHER ADVISORY PANEL

Helen Craddock
Infant School Headteacher

John Enticknap
Author and Primary School Headteacher

Arthur Razzell
Lecturer in Child Development,
Author and Headteacher

EDITORIAL BOARD

Philip M. Clark   Executive Editor
Rosemary Canter   Editor
Caroline Adams   Picture Researcher

DESIGNERS

Faulkner/Marks

ISBN 0333 252853 (vol 15)
0333 194446 (complete set)

© Macmillan Publishers Limited, 1980

First Published in 1980 by
Macmillan Children's Books
a division of Macmillan Publishers Limited
4 Little Essex Street, London WC2R 3LF
and Basingstoke

Associated companies in
New York, Toronto, Dublin,
Melbourne, Johannesburg and Delhi

Printed in Hong Kong

Outer Space

Contents

THE SOLAR SYSTEM

The earth we live on is a large ball of rock in space, called a planet. It circles round the sun with eight other planets. The sun with its planets is called the solar system. There are many smaller objects in space. These are called comets, asteroids, meteoroids and moons.

eclipse of the sun

sun

moon

earth

The earth goes round the sun.
The moon goes round the earth.
Sometimes the moon comes
between the sun and the earth.
Then we cannot see the sun.
This is called an eclipse of
the sun.

The sun

Our sun is really a star. It looks very
big and bright to us because it is
nearer to the earth than other stars.
It is a huge ball of hot gas.

Never look straight at the sun.
Never look at it through binoculars
or a telescope. Its light will burn
your eyes and blind you.

As we watch the sun it seems to rise in the morning, move across the sky, and sink at night. The sun is not really doing this. It is the earth that is spinning all the time. When our side of the earth faces the sun it is daytime. At night the sun shines on the other side of the earth. It never stops shining.

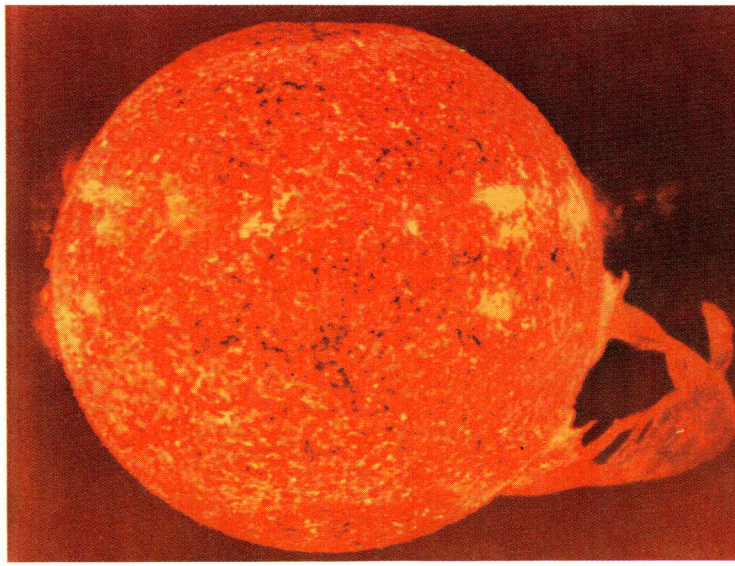

The sun is over 100 times larger than the earth. If the sun was the size of a football, the earth would be a pinhead.

This picture of the sun was taken from a space station called Skylab. You can see a huge curtain of gas that stretches out from the sun. This is made of cooler gas. The surface of the sun looks blotchy because the gas is always moving.

Mercury

Mercury is the nearest planet to the sun. It is very hot because it is so close to the sun. Nothing can live on it.

The Mariner spacecraft flew past Mercury taking photographs. Mercury looks like the moon. It is covered with craters and has no air.

Mercury

earth

Mercury is the smallest planet.
The earth is about three times
larger than Mercury.

Venus

We do not know much about Venus because it is hidden by thick clouds. Spacecraft like this Russian Venera have landed on Venus and sent back pictures. They show loose rocks lying on the ground. Venus is very hot.

Venus appears in the sky just before sunrise or just after sunset. It is called the 'morning star' or the 'evening star'.

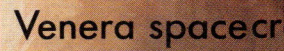

Venera spacecra

DAN ESCOTT

Venus

earth

Venus is the planet nearest to earth. It is almost the same size as earth. It is our sister planet.

The earth

The earth is the third planet from the sun. It is a round ball of rock covered with a layer of air called the atmosphere. The earth travels round the sun. This journey takes one year. The earth spins round all the time. Each spin takes a day and a night.

When the astronauts stood on the moon they saw the earth rise from behind the moon.

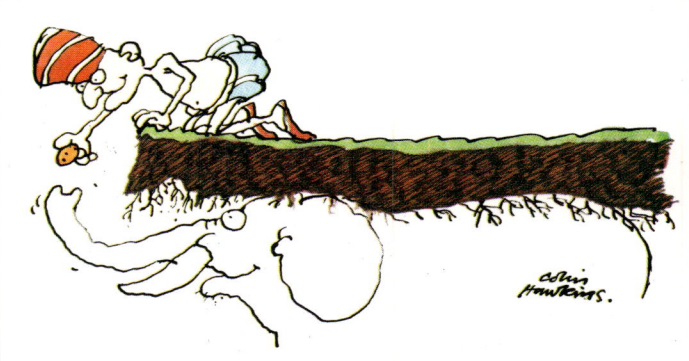

Many years ago people thought the earth was flat. In India people thought that an elephant carried the earth on its back.

This is what our planet looks like
from a spacecraft. It is mostly blue
sea with white wisps of cloud. Earth
is the only planet in the solar system
with oceans and seas. The brown
land you can see in this picture is
Africa and Arabia.

The moon

The moon is our nearest neighbour in space. It is still a very long way away. It moves round the earth but always keeps the same side towards us. We can only see this one side. There is no air or water on the moon. Billions of years ago rocks from space crashed onto the moon. They made craters all over it.

moon

Apollo astronauts made six trips to the moon. They walked on the surface and collected moon rocks to bring back to earth.

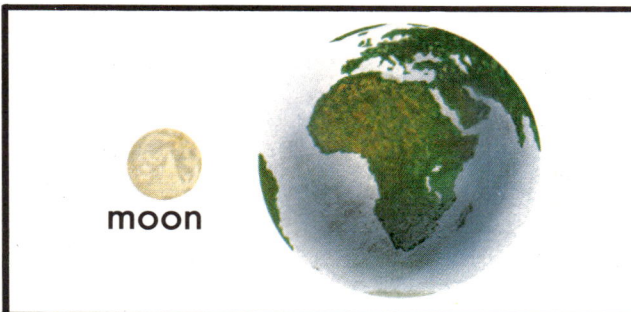

moon

The moon takes one month to go round the earth. The earth is about four times larger than the moon.

full moon

new moon

earth

half moon

half moon

sunlight

The sun shines on one side of the moon all the time. We see different amounts of the moon's bright side.

This footprint was left on the moon by one of the astronauts. It will stay there for thousands of years. There is no wind to blow it away and no water to wash it away.

Mars

Mars looks like a red star in the sky. The Viking spacecraft landed on Mars. It found that the rocky surface really is red. Mars is covered in red dust. Strong winds sometimes blow this into dust storms. There are very large volcanoes and valleys on Mars. They are much larger than any on earth.

This is a picture of sunset on Mars. The red dust is blown about by the winds. This makes the sky look pink.

Mars is a small planet. It has a thin layer of air. It is about half the size of the earth.

This picture of Mars was taken by a spacecraft. It is made up of lots of photographs joined together. That is why it looks patchy. The white part at the top is ice. It is rather like the arctic ice cap on earth. You can see a few clouds in the thin air around Mars.

Jupiter

Jupiter does not have a rocky surface. It is just a giant ball of liquid and gas. The coloured bands are clouds. They cover the whole planet. Jupiter has a red spot. It may be a storm that has lasted for hundreds of years.

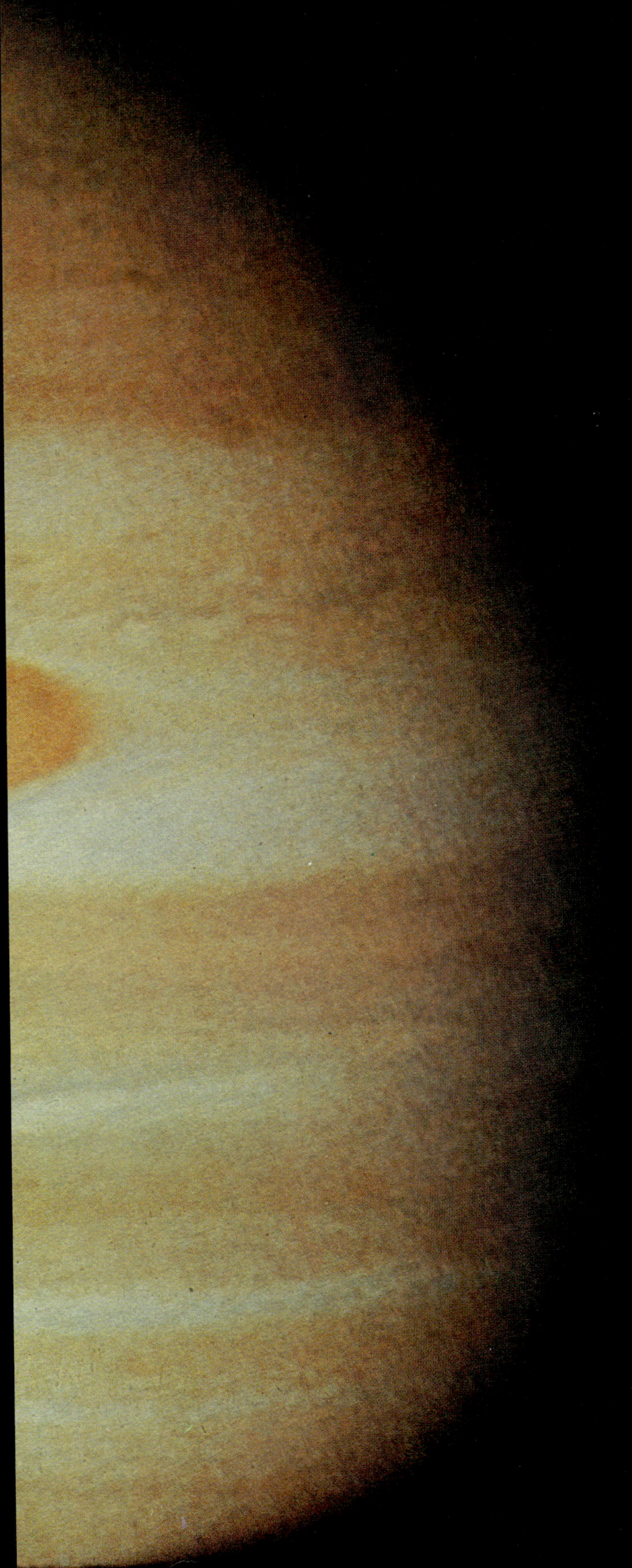

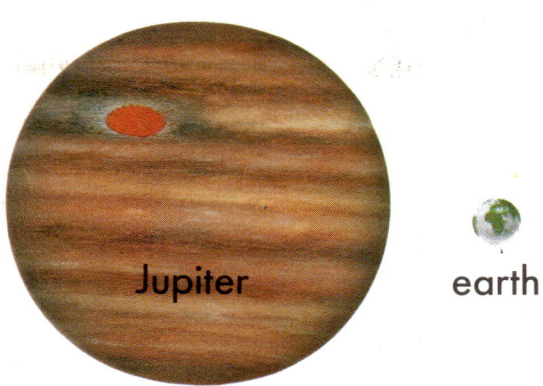

Jupiter   earth

Jupiter is the biggest planet that circles the sun. It is bigger than all the others put together.

moons

Jupiter has thirteen moons circling round it. Most of them are tiny chunks of rock. Four of the moons are larger. They are the same size as small planets.

Saturn

The sixth planet from the sun is Saturn. It is the farthest planet we can see without using a telescope. Saturn is like Jupiter in many ways. It is a big ball of liquid and gas. Coloured bands of cloud stretch round it. Saturn is spinning round very fast.

Very thin flat rings surround Saturn. Outside these rings there are ten moons circling round.

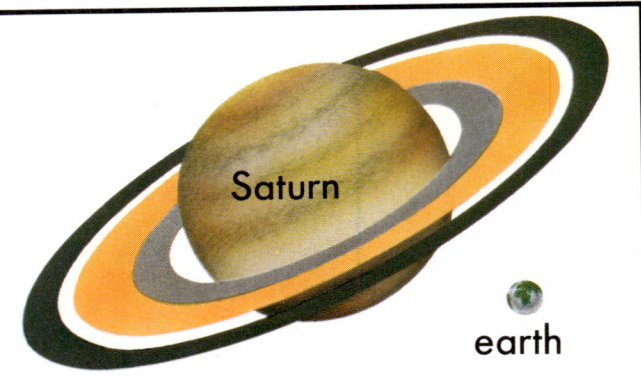

Saturn is a large planet. It is much bigger than the earth. Its rings reflect the sunlight. This makes Saturn look very bright.

The beautiful rings around Saturn are not solid. They are made of icy chunks of rock.

Uranus, Neptune and Pluto

We know little about these planets. They are very far away. Uranus and Neptune are liquid. They have thick cloudy atmospheres around them. Pluto may be a solid ball with an icy surface. All these planets are very cold. This is because they are a long way from the sun.

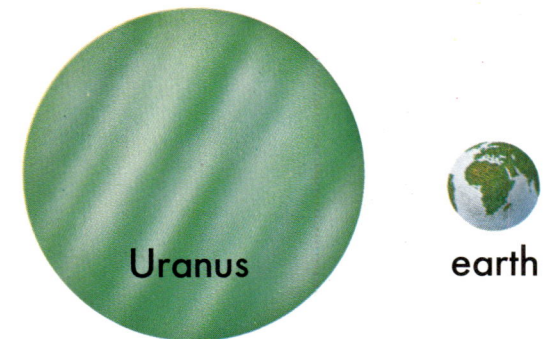
Uranus   earth

Uranus is much larger than the earth. It has five moons.

Herschel's telescope

When astronomers began to use telescopes to study the stars they discovered Uranus, Neptune and Pluto. Sir William Herschel discovered Uranus about 200 years ago. He used a telescope like this one. A few years ago astronomers first saw the rings round Uranus.

Many planets are named after the ancient gods. Uranus was the god of heaven.

Neptune is almost the same size as Uranus. It has two moons.

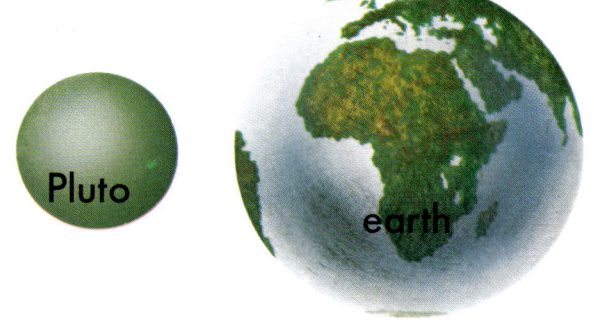

Pluto is a small planet. It is about the same size as Mercury.

The planet Neptune looks slightly blue. It was named after Neptune, the god of the sea.

Pluto was the god of the underworld. People thought you went there when you died.

Asteroids and meteors

Asteroids and meteors are pieces of rock. Asteroids circle round the sun. Meteors sometimes fall towards the earth. Small meteors burn up in our air. Some bigger ones called meteorites land on the earth. This one is in a museum. A very large meteorite made this crater when it landed in America.

meteorite

meteorite
crater

Comets

Bayeux
Tapestry

Comets are made of dust and ice. They come from the furthest part of the solar system. When they are near the sun they have huge bright tails. These people are watching a comet. Long ago people thought comets were unlucky. The Bayeux Tapestry was made 900 years ago. Can you see the comet?

THE UNIVERSE

The universe is the name we give to everything in space. The earth, the sun and all the planets are part of the universe. So are the stars we see at night. Astronomers see more stars than us with their telescopes. They are all part of the universe.

There are very thin clouds of dust and gas between the stars. The stars look blue because starlight shines on this dust.

Clouds of dust and gas are called nebulae. We can see them through a telescope. They look like dark patches in the sky. This is the Horsehead Nebula. It blocks out the light from stars behind it.

Horsehead Nebula

Stars

There are millions of stars in the universe. The stars we see in the sky at night are only a few of them. Stars are different sizes and different colours. They can be red, yellow, blue or white. They are all very far away. Some stars circle round other stars in pairs. Others are in large groups called clusters.

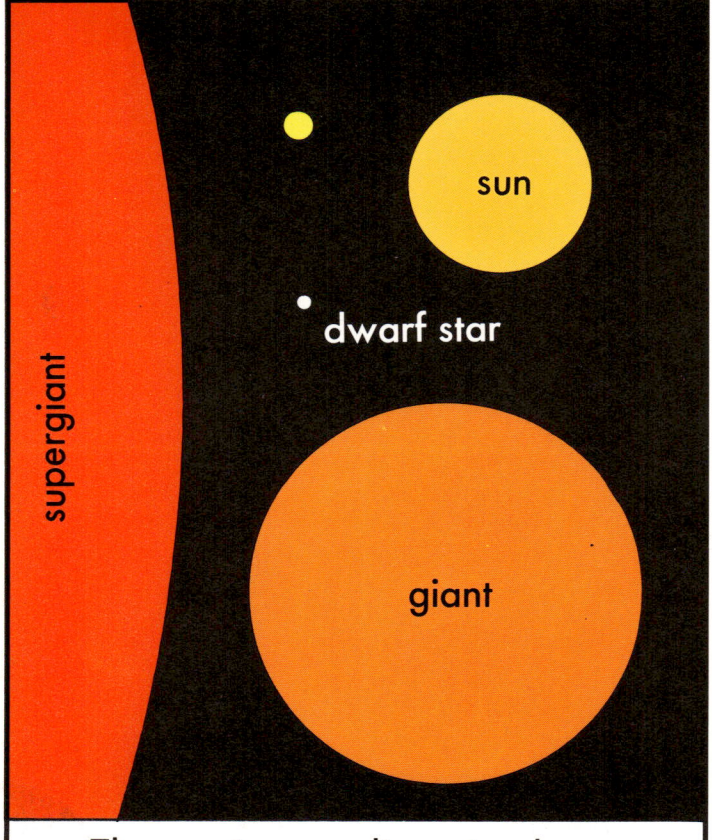

The sun is a medium sized star. It is in the middle of its life. Larger stars are called 'giants' and 'supergiants'. Smaller stars are called 'dwarf stars'.

cloud of gas

Some giant stars explode at the end of their lives. They suddenly shine very brightly. They are called supernovae.

Stars develop from a cloud of gas. This cloud draws together to make a ball of very hot gas. It starts to give out light and heat, like our own sun. After millions of years the gas gets used up. The star then grows bigger and redder. At last it shrinks to a tiny 'white dwarf' star. These changes take millions of years.

white dwarf star

Families of stars

The stars cling together in groups.
Each large group is called a galaxy.
When we look at the sky we can
see many stars. They are all in our
galaxy. On a clear night you can
see a faint band of light in the sky.
This light is called the Milky Way.
The stars near the middle of our
galaxy make this light.

Milky Way

Astronomers used to think that
our galaxy was the only one in
the universe. Now we know
there are many other galaxies.
They are very far away. Not all
are the same shape. Many
galaxies are spiral shaped.
Some galaxies are oval. Others
have no special shape.

Our galaxy is a flat spiral shape.
You can see a drawing of it above.
The sun is in one of the spiral arms.

This picture shows our galaxy from
the side. You can see the bulge in
the middle. The arrow shows where
we are.

our galaxy

How it all began

Nobody knows how the universe began. Scientists have tried to find out. Many scientists think the universe started with a big bang. There was a great explosion in space. This sent the galaxies spreading out in all directions. Scientists think the galaxies are still moving away from each other.

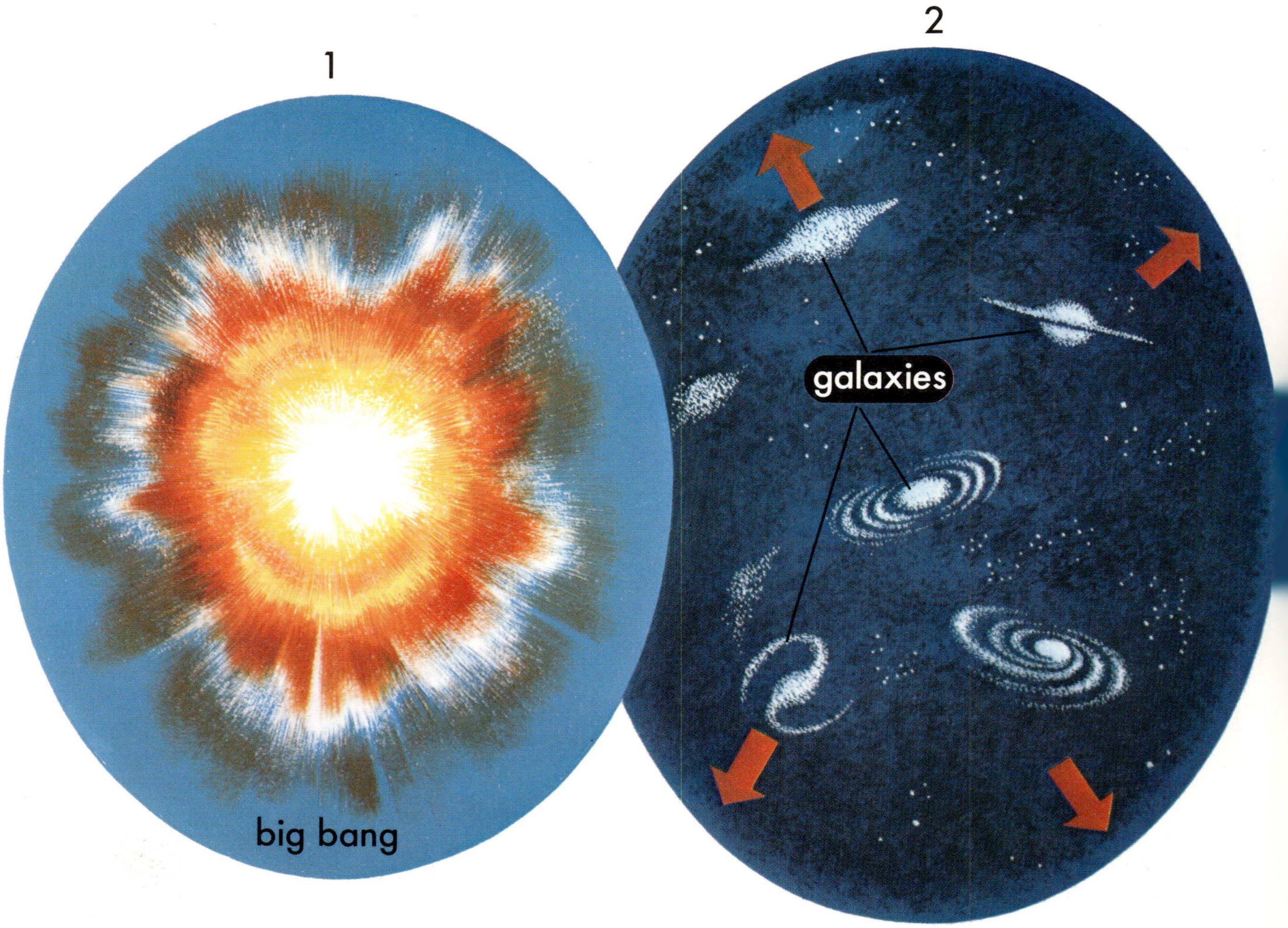

cloud of dust

sun

1

big bang

2

galaxies

planets

sun

People have tried to find out how the sun and its planets were made. Many scientists think the sun began as a spinning cloud of dust and gas. The gas collected at the centre and became the sun. The rest of the cloud kept spinning round the sun. The planets were made from this cloud.

3

4

Life in the universe

There are many kinds of plants and animals on earth. No living things have been found anywhere else in the solar system. People think there may be life in other parts of the universe. The stars are too hot for our kind of life. There may be life on other planets far away from our solar system.

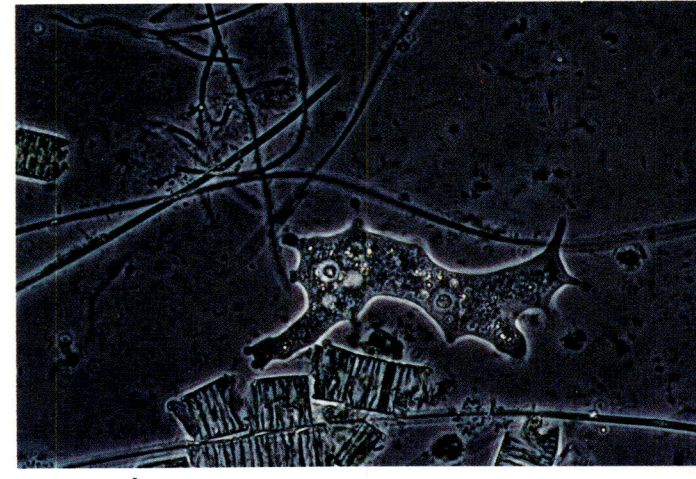
amoeba

There are many kinds of life on earth. The amoeba is tiny and very simple. Animals and people are much more complicated. There is life even in the most difficult places. The cactus can live in hot dry deserts. Bacteria can live even in the arctic. How many different kinds of life can you see in the middle picture?

cactus

Life on other planets may be
like these floating creatures or it
may be just simple plants.

plant on a rocky planet

ASTRONOMY

Astronomy is the study of all the stars and planets in the universe.

People have watched the sun, moon and planets for thousands of years. There is an ancient circle of stones at Stonehenge. It was probably built to help early astronomers. Galileo was the first person to look at the planets through a telescope. He was the first man to see the craters on the moon.

Stonehenge

Early telescopes were very small. This one was made by Sir Isaac Newton, a famous scientist. It is a bit smaller than this book.

early astronomers.

Telescopes

Telescopes help astronomers study the universe. They make planets look closer. This helps astronomers study the surface of the planets. Telescopes also make the stars look brighter. They help men see further in space too. With telescopes they can see many stars too far away for us to see with our eyes.

Big telescopes are needed to see distant stars. This telescope is much bigger than the man using it.

The radio telescope on the right picks up radio waves from space. It can study very distant stars.

The atmosphere around the earth
stops us seeing stars and planets
clearly. Scientists have built satellites.
These travel round the earth above
the atmosphere. This satellite studies
the sun.

The sky at night

People who live north of the earth's equator do not see exactly the same stars as people who live south of the equator. In Australia they can see the Southern Cross.

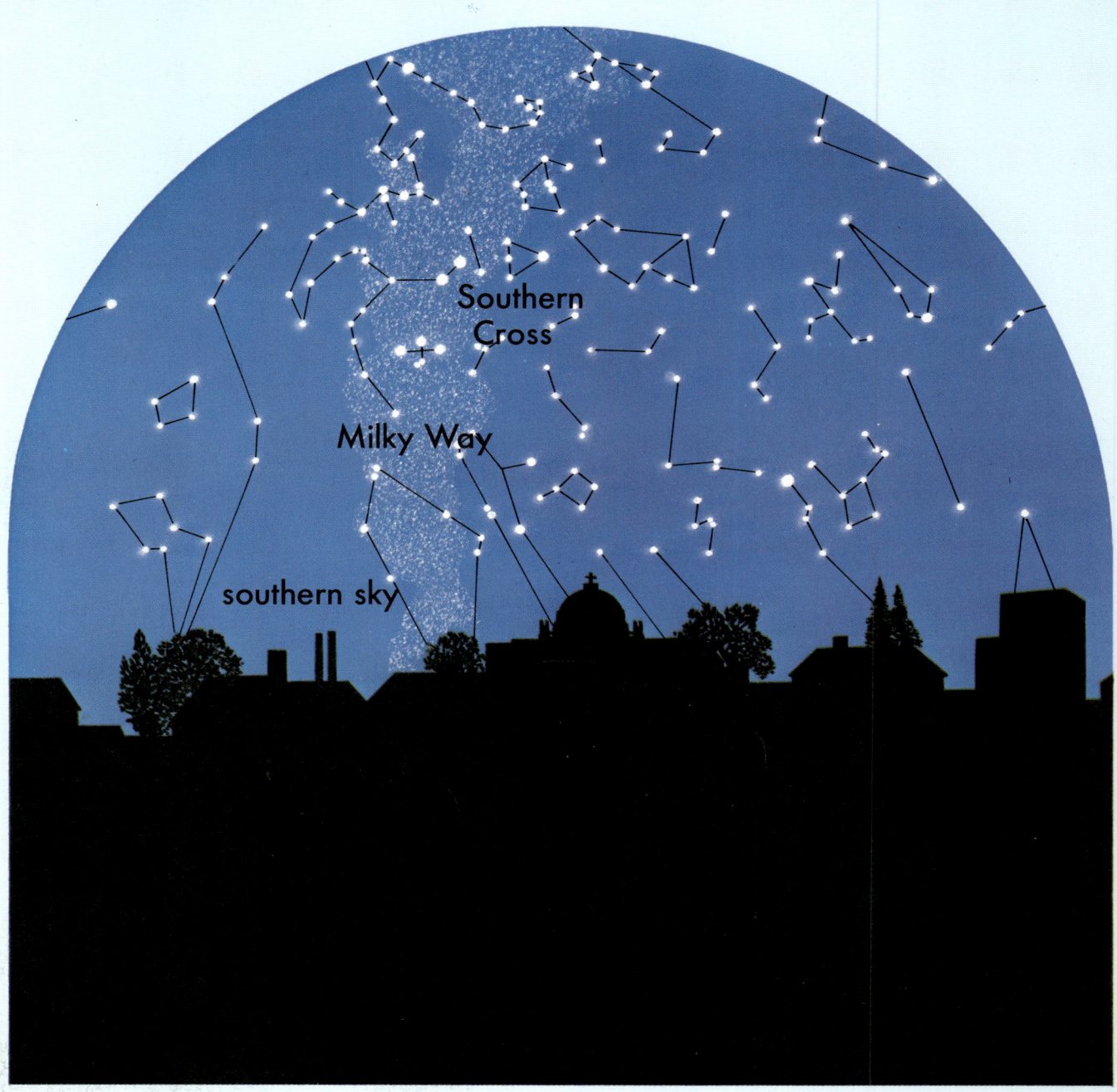

Southern Cross

Milky Way

southern sky

Long ago men gave names to groups of stars called constellations. The Great Bear is the easiest group to see in the northern sky. It has seven stars shaped like a plough.

Great Bear

Milky Way

northern sky

SPACE TRAVEL

Gravity is a strong force that keeps us on earth. Spacecraft have to travel very fast to escape the earth's gravity. They must fly more than 20 times faster than Concorde.

People cannot live in space without protection. They have to travel in spacecraft and wear spacesuits.

Spacecraft need powerful rockets to take them away from the pull of the earth's gravity. This huge Saturn V rocket sent men on their journey to visit the moon.

When a spacecraft comes back to earth it passes through the atmosphere. The spacecraft gets very hot. It has a thick skin called a heat shield to protect it. This American spacecraft landed in the sea.

spacecraft

Rockets

Spacecraft and satellites are launched by powerful rockets. Most of the rocket's weight is fuel. The spacecraft is only a tiny part near the rocket's nose. When the fuel is used up the rocket can no longer be used. A new rocket has to be built for each launch.

The V2 rocket was the first large rocket to be made. It was built in Germany. Space rockets were later developed from it.

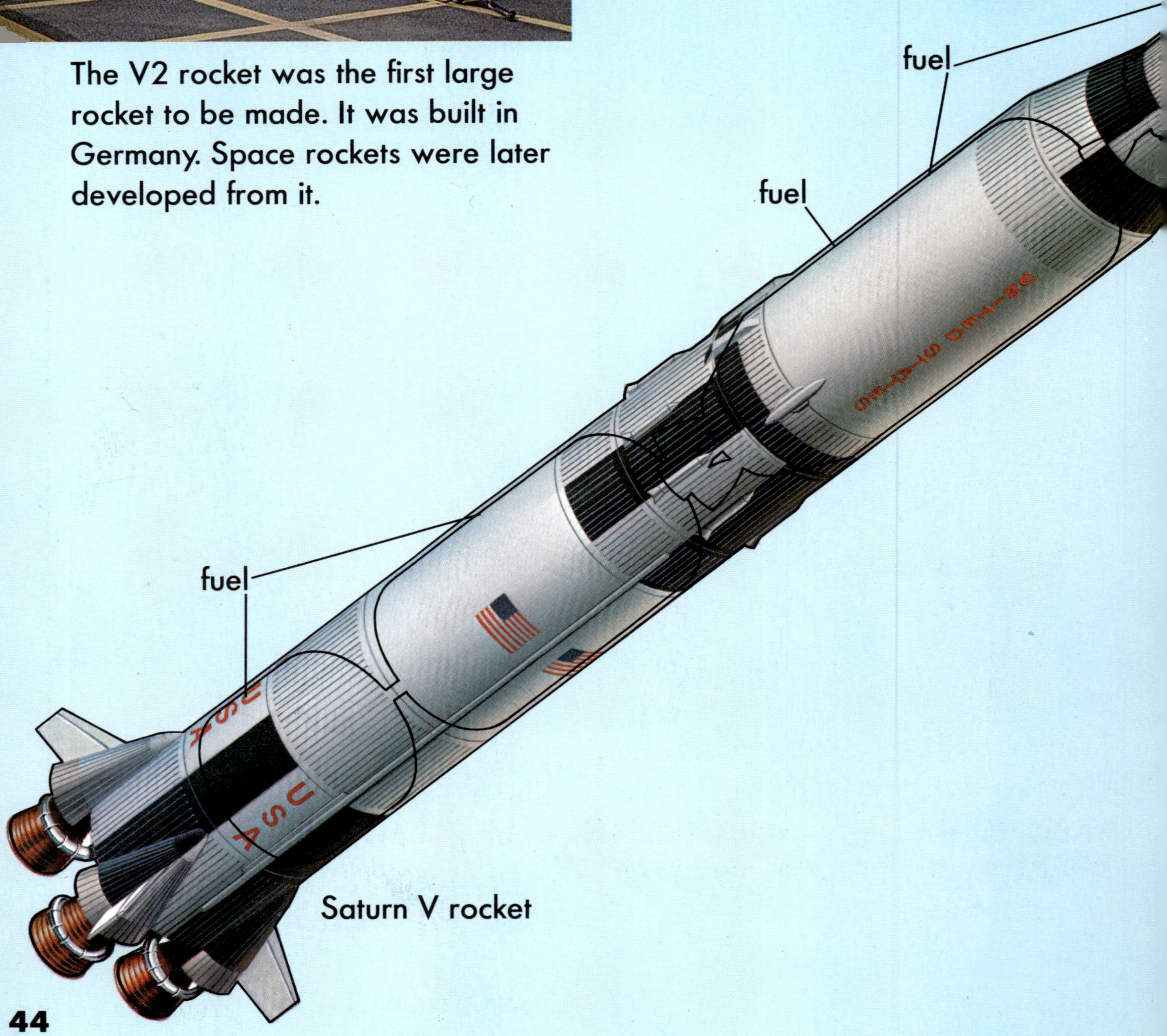

fuel

fuel

fuel

Saturn V rocket

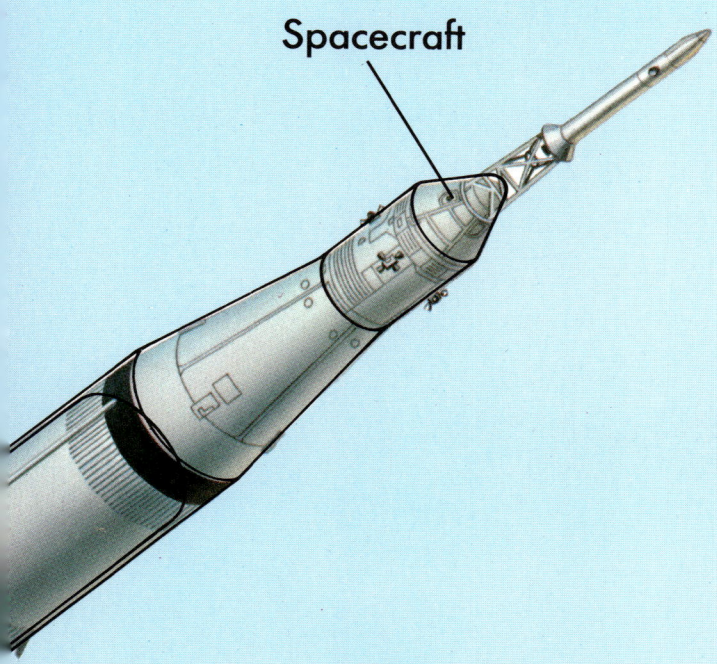

Spacecraft

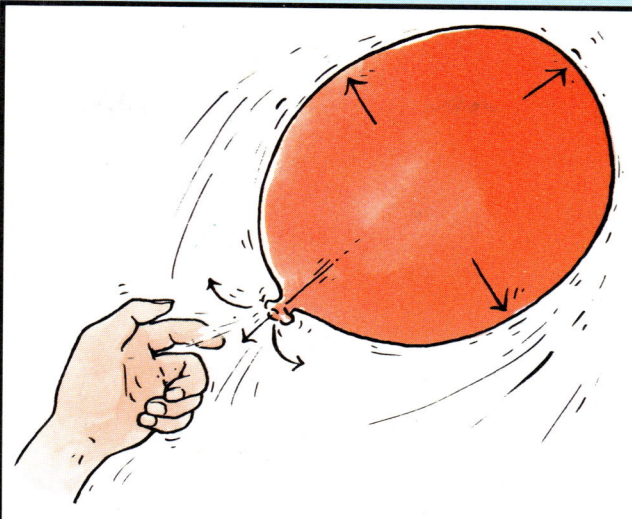

Blow up a balloon and let it go. It will fly away as the air rushes out. This is how a rocket works.

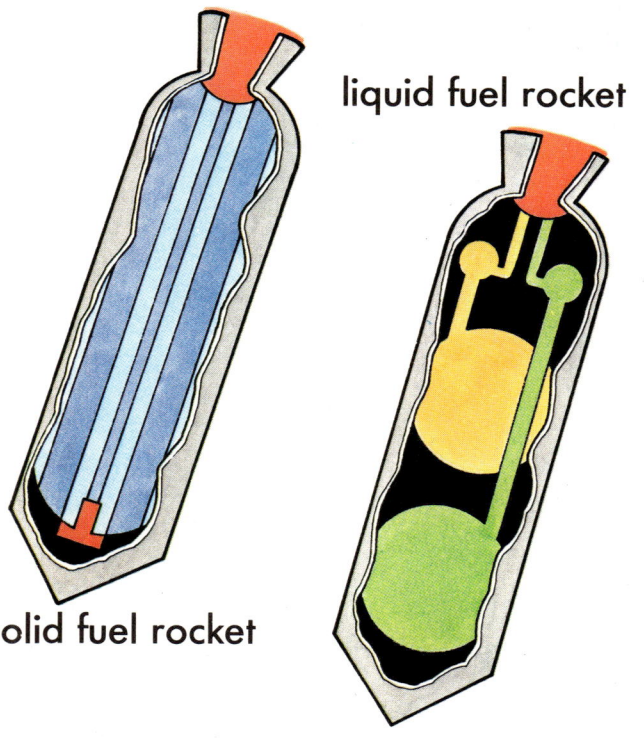

liquid fuel rocket

solid fuel rocket

When rocket fuel burns it makes hot gas. The gas shoots out pushing the rocket forward.

Robert Goddard built this strange early rocket. It was the first to use liquid fuel. At that time most people thought men would never be able to fly to the moon.

Satellites

Many satellites circle above the earth. Some study our weather to help the weather forecasters. Other satellites carry telephone messages to distant places. Some satellites send television pictures across the world. People in many countries can watch events like the Olympic Games as they are happening. Television cameras photograph the games. Satellites carry the pictures across the world.

satellite picture in America

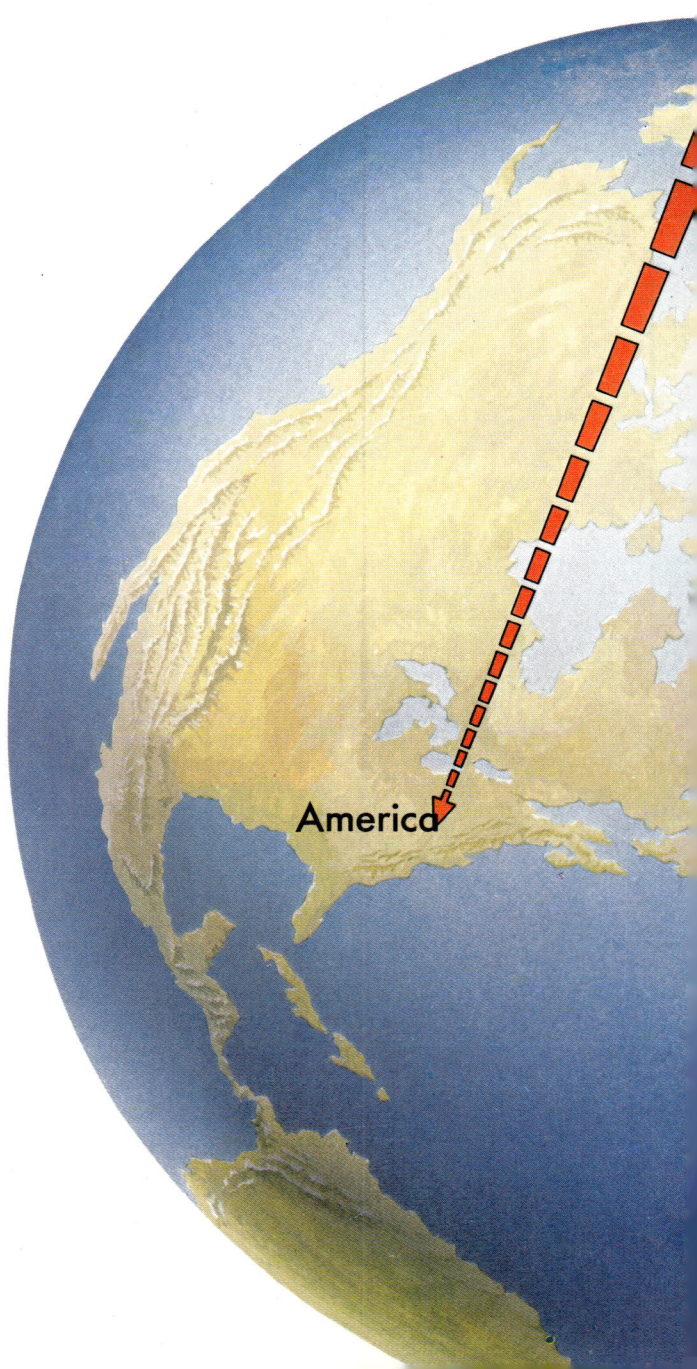

America

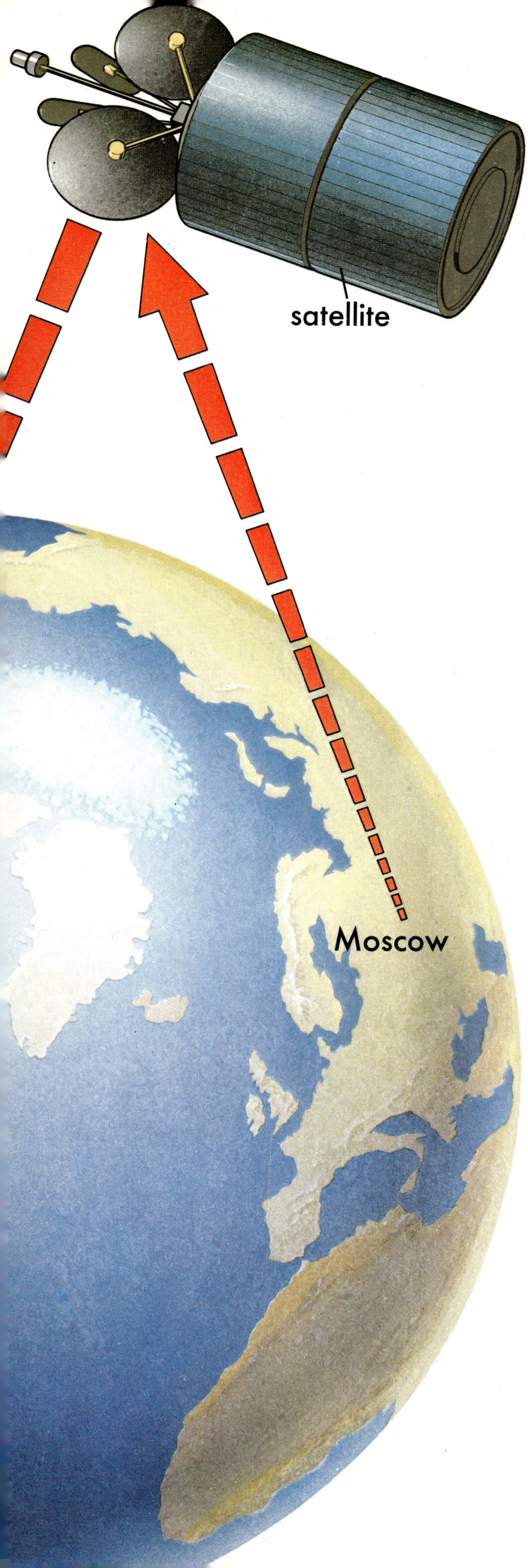

satellite

Invisible waves carry television pictures through the air. These waves travel in straight lines. They cannot bend round the earth's surface. A satellite is used to send pictures to distant countries.

The television pictures are sent up to a satellite. It bounces them back to earth. People in America can watch the Olympic Games being held in Moscow.

Moscow

Olympic games in Moscow

Man in space

There are many problems for men in space. There is no food or water and no air to breathe. The spacecraft must carry all these things to keep men alive. There is very little room inside a spacecraft. When the Apollo astronauts went to the moon they were squashed together, as you can see on the right.

Apollo astronaut

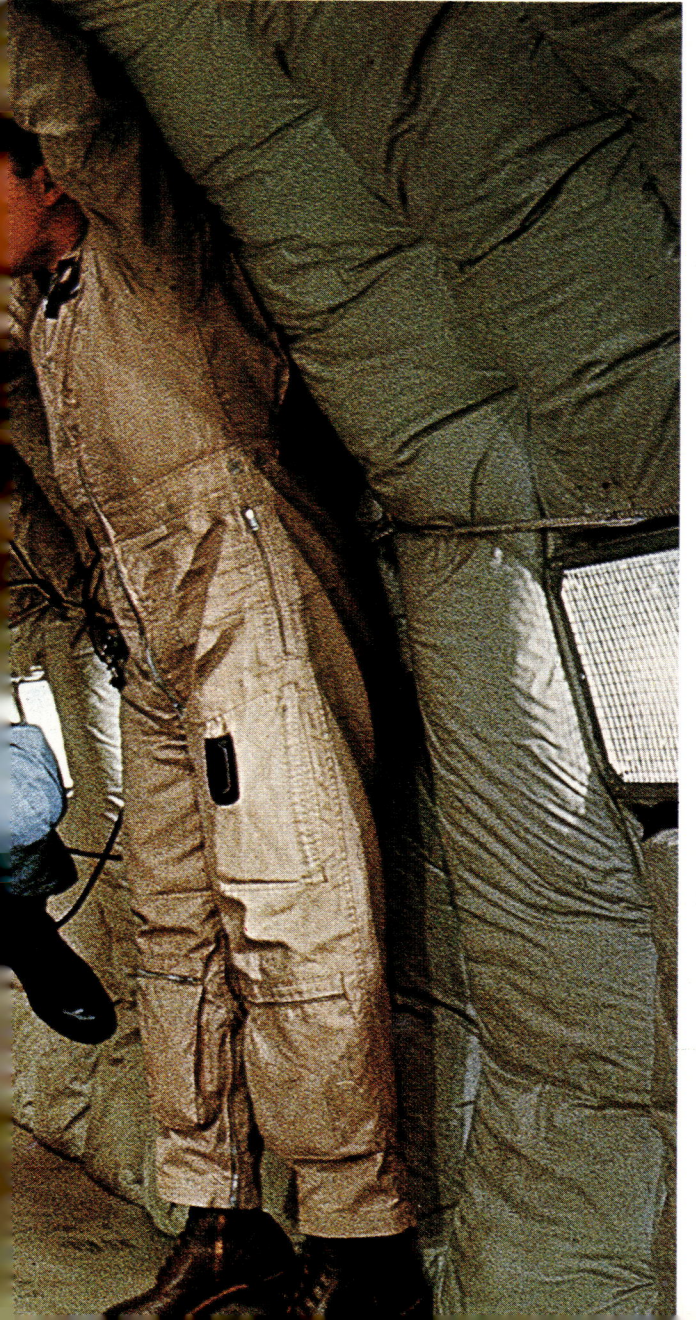

Astronauts must wear spacesuits if they go outside their spacecraft.

Everything floats in space. These astronauts are training in a special aircraft which makes them weightless.

Journey to the moon

A giant rocket launched three Apollo astronauts to the moon. They travelled in a small cabin in the nose of the spacecraft. This was called the Command Module. Near the moon two astronauts got into the Lunar Module. It took them to the moon's surface. The other man stayed in the spacecraft.

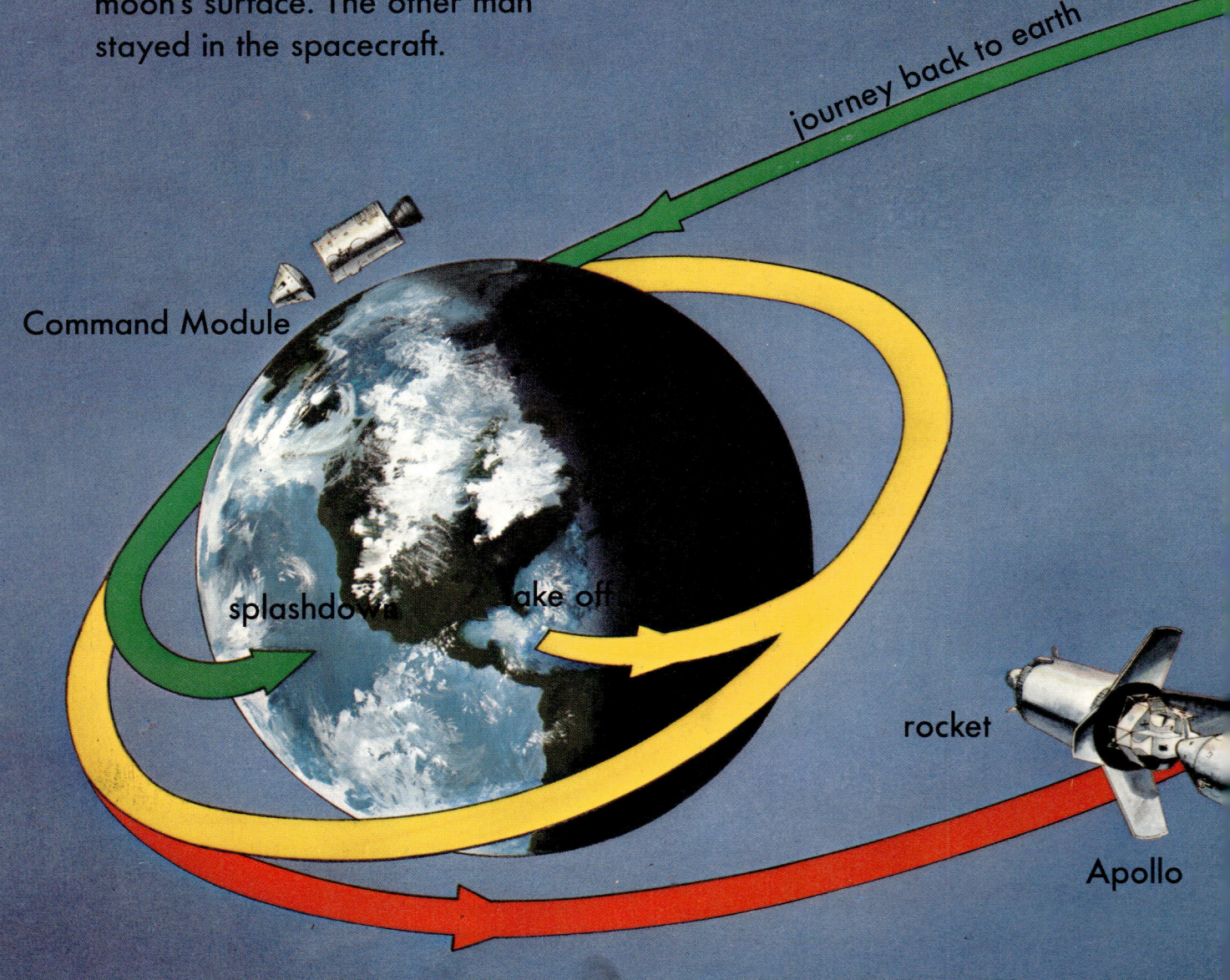

journey back to earth

Command Module

splashdown   take off

rocket

Apollo

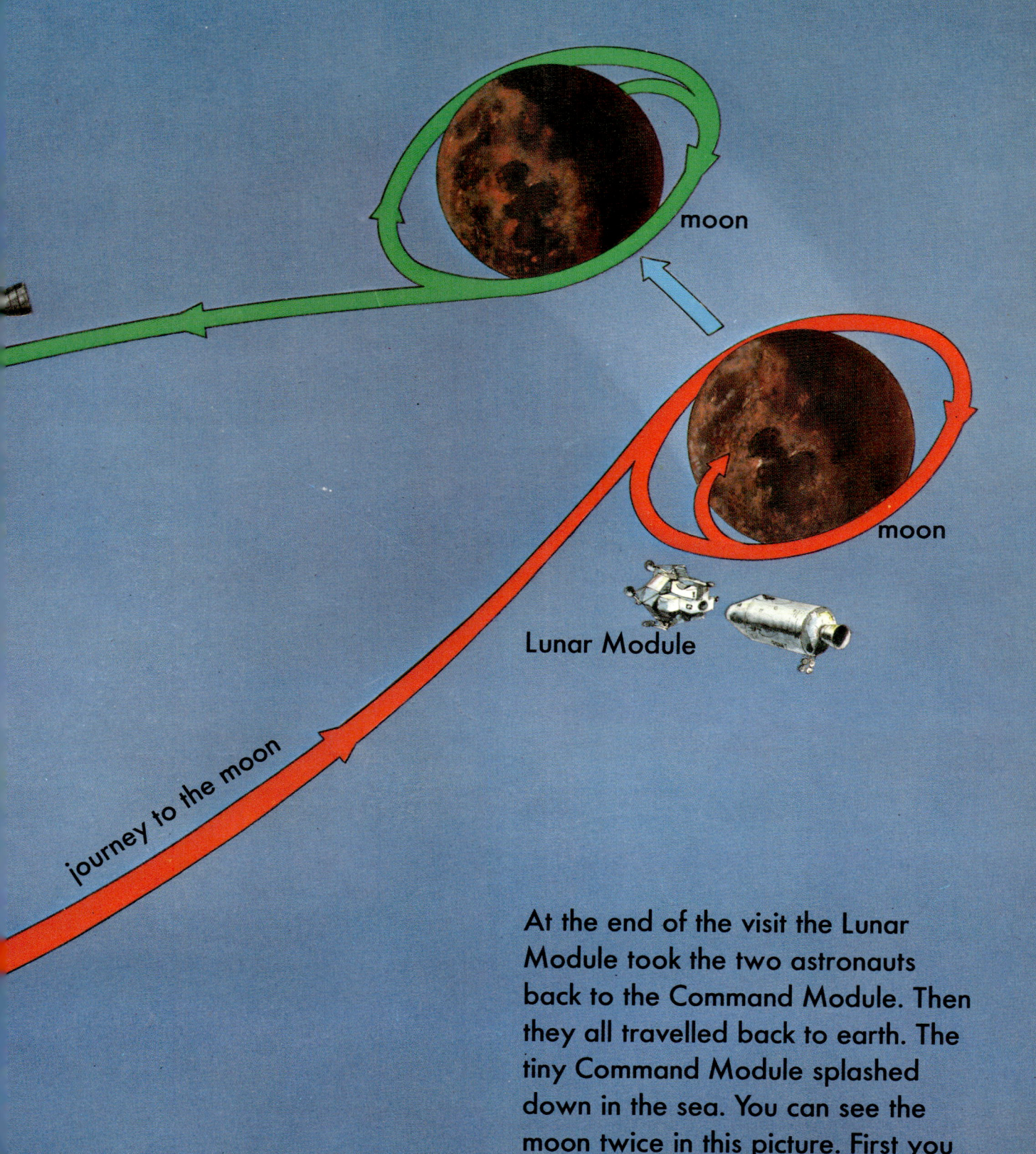

moon

moon

Lunar Module

journey to the moon

At the end of the visit the Lunar Module took the two astronauts back to the Command Module. Then they all travelled back to earth. The tiny Command Module splashed down in the sea. You can see the moon twice in this picture. First you can see the journey to the moon. Then you can see the journey back to earth.

Man on the moon

Twelve men have walked on the moon. They had to learn how to move on the moon's surface. This is not easy. Men weigh very little on the moon. It is easier for them to jump and hop than to walk. The men collected moon rocks to bring back to earth. Below you can see the earth behind the Apollo spacecraft.

Edwin Aldrin was the second man on the moon. He wore a special suit and carried air to breathe.

moon car

Lunar Module

On later trips astronauts took a moon car to help them travel.

The astronauts on the moon lived in the Lunar Module. It looked rather like a large spider.

Astronauts

The Americans call their spacemen astronauts. The Russians call their spacemen cosmonauts. In 1957 the Russians launched Sputnik. It was the first object to be sent into space. Four years later a Russian became the first man in space. His name was Yuri Gagarin. He flew once round the earth.

Yuri Gagarin

On the right is the American astronaut Ed White. He is walking in space. The cord joins him to the spacecraft. He is using a 'space gun' to push himself around. A Russian made the first spacewalk.

So far only one woman has flown in space. She is a Russian called Valentina Tereshkova. She circled the earth 48 times. Her flight lasted three days. Now there are women in America who are training to be astronauts.

Valentina Tereshkova

Astronauts must be fit and healthy. They have to train for many months. It is very expensive to send men into space. Unmanned spacecraft can do much of the work that is done by astronauts. Robot explorers can go further than men. They have visited five planets and landed on two of them.

Viking spacecraft

Robot explorers

Luna 16 is a Russian robot explorer. It scooped up soil from the moon and brought it to earth.

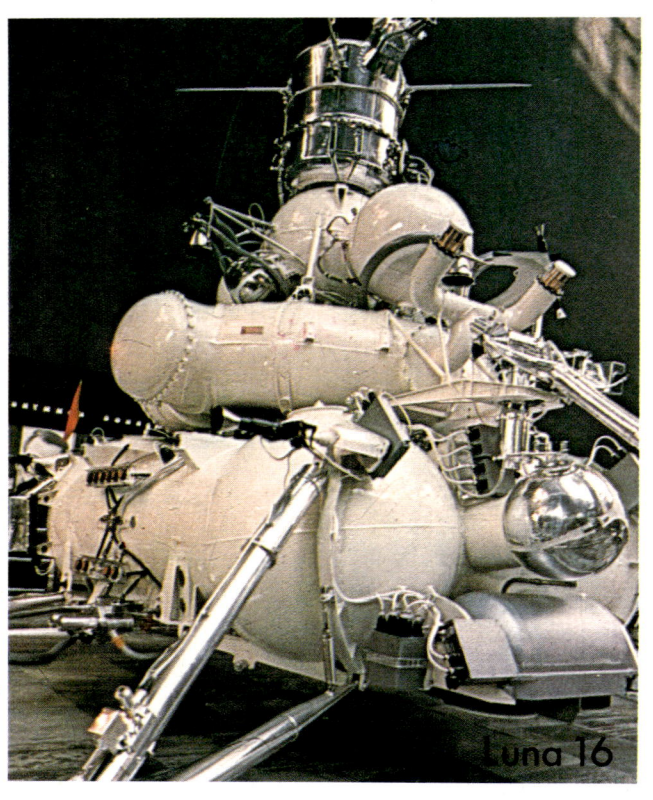

Luna 16

The Russian moon car above is called Lunokhod. Two of them were sent to the moon. They were controlled by scientists on earth. They crawled over the moon during the day. At night they closed down. They sent many exciting photographs of the moon back to scientists on earth.

Robot explorers have landed on the moon, Venus and Mars. The Viking spacecraft sent back pictures of Mars. Their robot explorers did not find any life there. This robot explorer is separating from the spacecraft and landing on Mars.

Mars

robot explorer

Space stations

Space stations are large spacecraft. Men can live and work in them for several months. They sleep in bunks and keep food from earth in the kitchen. There are workrooms and living areas. The men can live in comfort and wear ordinary clothes. The Skylab and Salyut space stations both circled the earth.

Spacecraft carry men to the space stations. This Russian Soyuz spacecraft is taking men up to the large Salyut space station.

Skylab was the first space station. It was damaged as it was launched. The first crew had to mend it before they could live in it.

Skylab

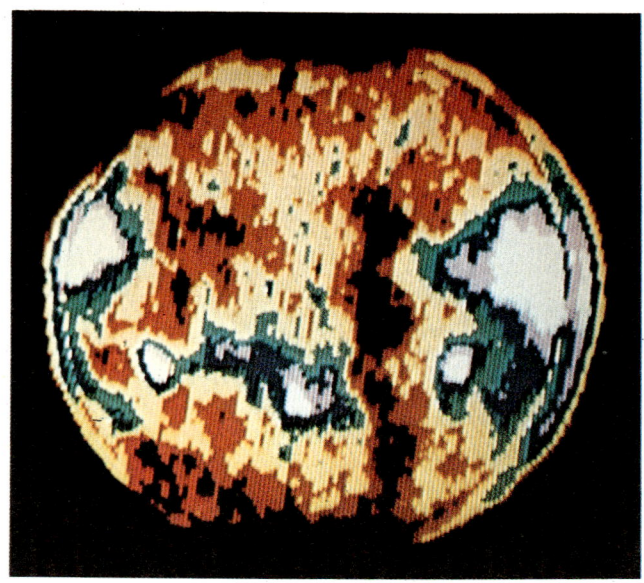

Nine astronauts lived in Skylab. They photographed the sun. A special camera took this picture of the sun. Cameras on earth cannot take photographs like this.

This is Skylab circling over the earth. The astronauts took a great many photographs of the earth. They also studied the clouds.

Space Shuttle

The Space Shuttle is a new type of spacecraft. It is a rocket plane that can be used many times. Booster rockets help it take off from earth. The Shuttle circles the earth while the people inside do their scientific work. Then it glides back to earth and lands on a runway like an ordinary aircraft.

Space Shuttle

booster rocket

rockets fall away

Shuttle take off

rockets land in sea

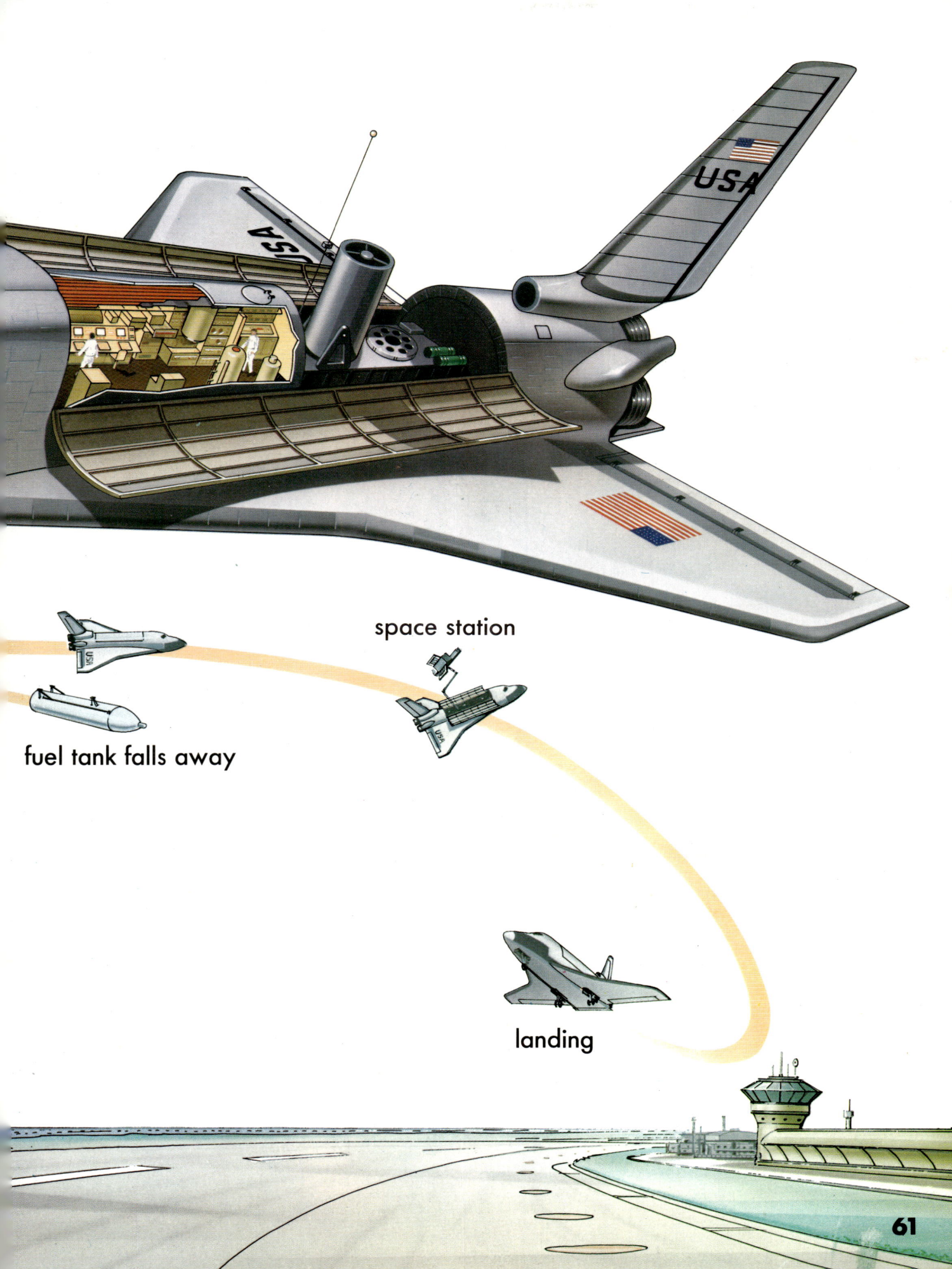

space station

fuel tank falls away

landing

The future

Men will continue to explore space. Perhaps they will visit other planets. Men may build places to live in on the moon or nearby planets.
It will be a long time before they can visit the stars. The nearest star is very far away. It would take thousands of years for a starship to reach it.

Space Shuttle

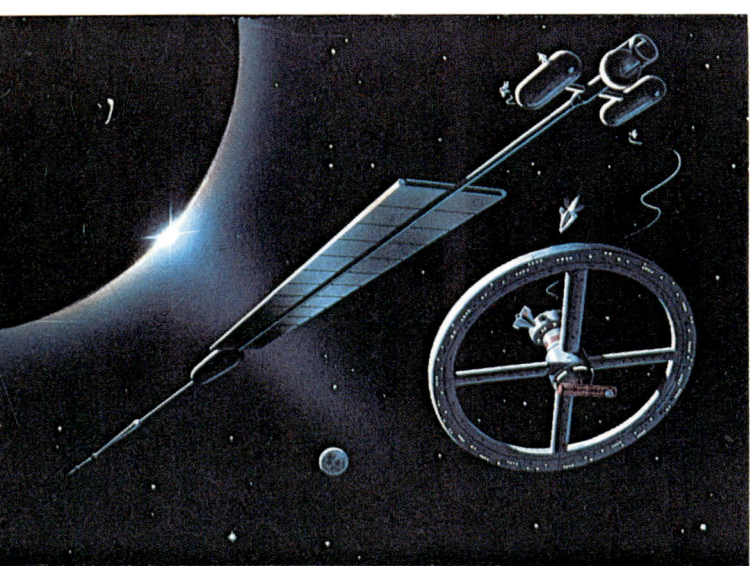

If the earth gets too crowded we may need to build homes in space. Perhaps one day some people will live on giant space stations circling round the earth.

The Space Shuttle could take men to space stations. These stations could collect energy from the sun. They could beam this energy back to earth for people to use.

space station

63

DID YOU KNOW?

The first living creature in space was a Russian dog called Laika. She lived in space for seven days. The Russians used her to find out what happened to living things in space. Monkeys, mice, spiders and frogs have also been sent in spacecraft. They helped scientists learn about space travel.

The first close-up picture of another planet was taken in 1965. The Mariner 4 spacecraft flew past Mars and photographed it.

About 10,000 man-made objects have now been sent into space. Almost half of them are still there.

INDEX